Growing Readers

New Hanover County Public Library

Purchased with
New Hanover County Partnership for Children
and Smart Start Funds

D1710325

What's Awake?

What's Awake?
123

Patricia Whitehouse

Heinemann Library
Chicago, Illinois

Customer Service 888-454-2279
Visit our website at www.heinemannlibrary.com

Designed by Sue Emerson, Heinemann Library
Printed and bound in the United States by Lake Book Manufacturing, Inc.

07 06 05 04 03
10 9 8 7 6 5 4 3 2 1

Library of Congress Cataloging-in-Publication Data
Whitehouse, Patricia, 1958-
    What's awake 123 / Patricia Whitehouse.
        p. cm. — (What's awake)
Includes index.
Summary: Portrays nocturnal animals including a bat, a rat, and a coyote.
    ISBN: 1-58810-885-6 (HC), 1-40340-631-6 (Pbk.)
1. Counting—Juvenile literature. 2. Nocturnal animals—Juvenile literature. [1. Nocturnal animals. 2 Counting.] I. Title.
QA113. W496 2002
513.2'11   2001008297

Acknowledgments
The author and publishers are grateful to the following for permission to reproduce copyright material:
p. 4 Jeff Lepore/Photo Researchers, Inc.; p. 5 Len Rue, Jr./Photo Researchers, Inc.; p. 7 Joe McDonald/Visuals Unlimited; p. 9 Ray Coleman/Visuals Unlimited; pp. 11, 13, 17 Stephen Dalton/Photo Researchers, Inc.; p. 15 Terry Whittaker/Photo Researchers, Inc.; p. 19 Gilbert Twiest/Visuals Unlimited; p. 21 Tom & Pat Leeson/Photo Researchers, Inc.; p. 22 Erin Cross/Visuals Unlimited

Cover photograph by (L-R) Len Rue, Jr./Photo Researchers, Inc.; J. L. Lepore/Photo Researchers, Inc.; and Stephen Dalton/Photo Researchers, Inc.

Every effort has been made to contact copyright holders of any material reproduced in this book.
Any omissions will be rectified in subsequent printings if notice is given to the publisher.

Special thanks to our advisory panel for their help in the preparation of this book:

Eileen Day, Preschool Teacher
Chicago, IL

Ellen Dolmetsch,
Library Media Specialist
Wilmington, DE

Kathleen Gilbert,
Teacher
Round Rock, TX

Sandra Gilbert,
Library Media Specialist
Houston, TX

Angela Leeper,
Educational Consultant
North Carolina Department
of Public Instruction
Raleigh, NC

Pam McDonald, Reading Teacher
Winter Springs, FL

Melinda Murphy,
Library Media Specialist
Houston, TX

The publisher would also like to thank Dr. Dennis Radabaugh, Professor of Zoology at Ohio Wesleyan University in Delaware, Ohio, for his help in reviewing the contents of this book.

The sun goes down.

You are getting ready to go to sleep.

Some animals are waking up.

First   1st

The first animal is
a coyote.

It lifts its head to howl.

Second   2nd

The second animal is a raccoon.

It is climbing a tree.

Third   3rd

The third animal is an opossum.

It carries two baby opossums on its back.

baby opossum

Fourth   4th

The fourth animal is a bat.

It flies around eating bugs.

11

Fifth   5th

The fifth animal is a rat.

Rats eat garbage.

Sixth   6th

The sixth animal is another rat.

This rat is chewing on a deer antler.

Seventh   7th

The seventh animal is a barn owl.

It is looking for mice.

Eighth   8th

The eighth animal is a dog.

It is chasing a skunk.

Ninth   9th

The ninth animal is
a skunk.

It lifts its tail to spray
the dog.

Tenth   10th

The tenth animal is a woman calling her dog.

Sometimes dogs and people wake up at night.

Quiz

Which animal did you see first?

Note to Parents and Teachers

Learning ordinal numbers is a basic math skill. *What's Awake? 123* helps children learn sequencing with ordinal numbers using nocturnal animals as examples. You can help children make ordinal numbers a part of their math vocabulary by making them a part of your everyday talk. For example, as children line up to go outside you might ask them to tell you who is first in line, who is second, and so on. Alternatively, you could ask children to help you put groceries away at home. You might give them instructions to put the bananas away first, the apples second, the pears third, and so on.

! **CAUTION:** Remind children that it is not a good idea to handle wild animals. Children should wash their hands with soap and water after they touch any animal.

Index

Answer to page 23

1st   **2nd**   **3rd**

24